21st Century
Basic Skills
Library

WE CELEBRATE KWANZAA IN WINTER

by Rebecca Felix

Cherry Lake Publishing • Ann Arbor, Michigan

1

Published in the United States of America
by Cherry Lake Publishing
Ann Arbor, Michigan
www.cherrylakepublishing.com

Consultant: Marla Conn, ReadAbility, Inc.
Editorial direction and book production: Red Line Editorial

Photo Credits: Jupiterimages/liquidlibrary/Thinkstock, cover, 1, 10, 12, 14;
Tim Nichols/iStockphoto/Thinkstock, 4; Hill Street Studios/Blend Images/
AP Images, 6; Creatas/Thinkstock, 8; Vstock LLC/Thinkstock, 16; Hill Street
Studios/Blend Images/Corbis, 18; Purestock/Thinkstock, 20

Library of Congress Cataloging-in-Publication Data
Felix, Rebecca, 1984-
  We celebrate Kwanzaa in winter / by Rebecca Felix.
      pages cm. -- (Let's Look at Winter)
  Includes index.
  ISBN 978-1-63137-611-5 (hardcover) -- ISBN 978-1-63137-656-6 (pbk.) --
  ISBN 978-1-63137-701-3 (pdf ebook) -- ISBN 978-1-63137-746-4 (ebook)
  1. Kwanzaa--Juvenile literature. I. Title.

GT4403.F45 2013
394.2612--dc23

                                2014004567

Cherry Lake Publishing would like to acknowledge the work of The
Partnership for 21st Century Skills. Please visit www.p21.org for more
information.

Printed in the United States of America
Corporate Graphics Inc.
July 2014

TABLE OF CONTENTS

Seven Days

Kwanzaa is an African American holiday. It lasts seven days. It starts December 26.

People **celebrate** seven **principles**. Families talk about one each day.

Kinaras

People use seven **symbols**.
One is a **kinara**.

What Do You See?

What colors are the candles?

Kinaras hold seven candles. People light a new one each night.

What Do You See?

What is on the mat?

Mats

People set out straw mats. They set corn and other symbols on them.

People set out a special cup.
They drink from it.

What Do You See?

What foods do you see?

Give and Eat

People eat special foods.

Many people give gifts. Some dress up.

Kwanzaa ends January 1. People gather. They share a meal. It is a time of **unity**.

Find Out More

BOOK

Aloian, Molly. *Kwanzaa*. New York: Crabtree, 2009.

WEB SITE

Kwanzaa—Primary Games
www.primarygames.com/holidays/kwanzaa/kwanzaa.htm
Learn more about Kwanzaa with fun games and printouts.

Glossary

celebrate (SEL-uh-brate) to enjoy an event or holiday with others

kinara (kee-NAR-uh) a special candleholder used for Kwanzaa

principles (PRIN-suh-puhlz) laws or beliefs

symbols (SIM-buhlz) objects that are used to stand for or remember something

unity (YOO-nit-ee) being happily joined as one group

Home and School Connection

Use this list of words from the book to help your child become a better reader. Word games and writing activities can help beginning readers reinforce literacy skills.

African	each	kinara	seven
American	eat	Kwanzaa	share
candles	ends	lasts	special
celebrate	families	light	starts
colors	foods	mats	straw
corn	gather	meal	symbols
cup	gifts	new	talk
days	give	night	time
December	hold	people	unity
dress	holiday	principles	use
drink	January	set	

What Do You See?

What Do You See? is a feature paired with select photos in this book. It encourages young readers to interact with visual images in order to build the ability to integrate content in various media formats.

You can help your child further evaluate photos in this book with additional activities. Look at the images in the book without the What Do You See? feature. Ask your child to describe one detail in each image, such as a food, activity, or setting.

Index

About the Author

Rebecca Felix is an editor and writer from Minnesota. Many people celebrate Kwanzaa there. Families and friends gather in homes. People gather in cities to celebrate with dance, music, and food.